Finding The Lights On

D1526070

Finding The Lights On

Robert Hilles

For Sarah

in exchange
good luck with your
own work though 93
and on

Vt Holl
6/19/93

Wolsak and Wynn . Toronto

Many of these poems have appeared or will appear in *Antigonish Review, Arc,
Ariel, Blue Buffalo, Canadian Literature, CVII, Event, Fiddlehead, Grain, The Malahat
Review, NewWest Review, Poetry Canada Review, Prairie Fire, Prairie Journal of
Canadian Literature, SansCrit, University of Windsor Review*, and in the anthology
Men and Women (Together and Alone), published by The Spirit That Moves Us.

I wish to thank the editors of these magazines for the help they have given me.

Cover art "Mother and Child" by Carole Bondaroff of Heart Studios, Calgary.
Photograph by Norbert Gousseau.
Typeset in Palatino, printed in Canada by
The Coach House Press, Toronto.

The author wishes to thank the Alberta Foundation for the Literary Arts and
The Canada Council for their financial support. The publishers gratefully
acknowledge support by The Canada Council and The Ontario Arts Council.

Wolsak and Wynn Publishers Ltd.
Don Mills Post Office Box 316
Don Mills, Ontario, Canada, M3C 2S7

Canadian Cataloguing in Publication Data
Hilles, Robert, 1951-
  Finding the lights on
Poems.
ISBN 0-919897-27-4
I. Title.
PS8565.I48F5 1991   C811'.54   C91-095216-7
PR9199.3.H55F5 1991

For my mother Hazel and for Rebecca

CONTENTS

FINDING THE LIGHTS ON

LETTERS TO MY MOTHER

LETTER I

Today the water tastes bad. I read a book last night
but I can remember nothing except its cover. The pages
silent, disappeared into the darkness over my
shoulder. I thought of your madness and suddenly I
wanted to take your place, leave aside the noble
gestures of doubt. And I wondered what language is this
that allows me to tremble, to not listen when a door
opens that makes me think of you standing in the middle
of a lake waving. When I was younger I wanted you to
forget about other languages. I wanted you to stop
hearing my words, to think of me as an antidote for the
other voices you couldn't shut out. Instead, you started
a fire and warmed your hands, made me a cup of tea and
smiled, turned away, as though my face was that of a
stranger.

Am I wrong to blame language now or the tongue that
licks its way inside you?

When I read to you this letter, you will not hear it
because the words will vanish at my tongue; the tongue
I cut out for you so you could hear me without
language, without the convenient flame of syllables. Then
you would see how I loved you first because my body
told me. How language is the room we all enter by
accident and never leave.

The questions I ask you now are different, wilder, more
daring the result of sitting all night in the dark,
hearing your words in my head, simple words, words that
never stop, no matter how hard I close my eyes.
I send you this single flower, in its petals you will
see a new language form, one you can use without
hurting yourself.

LETTER II

Some mornings the sunrise is so pure I want to stop it
before it can move on. Last week it rained in December,
and I thought of you alone in your basement apartment,
phoning friends or relatives to make the days pass. I
wanted to write but couldn't, caught in a faculty
meeting. I should have told you about the sunrise how
it never chooses the same window to appear in and
passes despite my attempts. Instead, I played an old
tape of yours, listened to it hiss like your breathing.
Today when I mailed this it had stopped raining. I
waited at the curb while the light was red and I felt
the sunrise grow inside me, felt my hands tremble as
they tossed the envelope into oblivion. In your reply,
be gentle, but precise. I don't want to hear about rain
or snow or sunrise. I want to smell you on the envelope,
to see your life flattened onto the page, to hear you
swear for the first time, your pen shaking.

LETTER III

Today, I cannot write but I must. I awoke three times
last night and I heard you scream as though you were in
the next room. When I called this morning, you were out
visiting a neighbour. I am older now than you were on
the day I was born and I can't imagine myself as a
child. In Breanne, I see the mistakes that children
make, see the promise that each morning makes to them.
On nights like last night, when the terror is so real,
it is death that I think of, unsure how to listen to the
darkness and still go on living. I trembled and tried
to hold you in my mind, counted the days to your
birthday, promised to write to you truthfully for a
change. However, sleep eventually came and with it the
smooth wash of amnesia. I write anyway, although in the
morning it all seems silly, too exaggerated by the
lateness of the hour and the quiet. This morning, the
traffic outside the window is an easy distraction and I
turn away from this letter abandoning it, like so many
others that I find impossible to finish.

LETTER IV

I heard you dreaming this morning and turned to one
side expecting to see you near the stove or at the
sink. A silly thing to expect after all these years
apart. But you are there, hunched over as you were so
often when I was a child. Your spirit breaking a little
more with each day. You sing every night or lie on your
bed reading a book. Our lives filled with the images of
others alone. You are in many of my dreams. Sometimes
too young to be my mother, you walk down the street and
cars full of maniacs pass yelling nasty things. As I
wash the dishes at night, I think of your hands, how
they never wrinkle but stay young, defying the
duties they accepted. I am tone deaf, my voice raw
unable to shape the roundness of melody as yours is, with
so little effort. Our gifts are accidental, discovered
on a morning alone near a window as the rest of the
world seems preoccupied with itself. This letter can
not explain what I have learned by listening to you
sing alone on a cold winter's night. Just the two of us
pretending to be the whole world. Those are the nights
I will never forget, those are the nights we both carry
with us now, cities apart but joined by a single
loneliness.

LETTER V

I want to undo us. To come back down the path that
words have lead us. To stop at a particular date and
swerve away from the known. Do it over wrong or right.
For words have carried us too deep into our lives. What
is left is not enough. I made my choices too quickly,
abandoned you because you were my mother and I wanted
to find the limits of your love. We need to search
within for god's long pause.

I come back and you are not home. Dad is washing the
car, cats hide beneath the house while I poke around. I
say nothing but leave calmly already half-way to town
before I realize where you are.

All I can send you is a single word wrapped in an
envelope. "Love". Spelling doesn't matter nor the heat of
the pen. My life ends when there are no more letters to
mail.

The trees in the back yard have no leaves and winter
lasts a very long time.

LETTER VI

After our move to this new house, you help unpack our
new life. I see the places in my house that are
occupied by you. I can measure your effect on them,
can learn the corners of the kitchen you have claimed,
spices ordered in a way I would not have chosen. In the
living room a picture appears that I cannot place.
These are your final whispers to me on a warm summer's
day. I have no way to free these places, to let them
slowly return to me, become mine again, altered only
inside me.

LETTER VII

Where are you now? I try to find you but can't. You say
that is how sons are. When I do find you, I will
disappear again into the rain, leaving the door open
behind me.

And is this an opera? I ask myself some nights, listen
as our teeth try to explain us. There is definitely a
plot but it does not exist. We are trained to run in
circles and obey the light.

I write these letters in places you want to visit but
can't. I stay in hotels you ask me about. Their
descriptions are enclosed. From the highest window, I
watch you walk the beach. There is no point in waving
because you do not know that I am there. When I mail
this, I will already be at home finishing the last
pages of a book, the neighbour's dog sniffing through
the garbage. Children playing bravely in the street.

LETTER VIII

The first separation was the hardest: son from mother.
Suddenly two fleshes, not one. The others started when I
was eight. The first time you ran away cursing dad for
the voices in your head. We ended up at the Salvation
Army and I hated them because they did not understand
your words, did not see that you were my mother and it
was okay for you to rant on as long as you were there.
They didn't know the isolation you had suffered, alone
with no friends, hiding in the bush.

Eventually the police took you away in a small brown
car. I cried. I hated my father too, could not face his
gentle confusion. He shook inside, but I couldn't see
it. Could only see your face in the car window looking
back as though your life was disappearing into the eyes
of your children. My brother, too young to understand,
waved as if you were going on a visit to your sisters.

At the Salvation Army my sister, who was only a year
old, needed a bottle and they warmed one for her while
you sat in a ball crying, calling out God and Satan's
names as though they were your children's names. I
could hear the minister talking to my father on the
phone, and I hated everyone except you. Your tears
seemed to be the world. Turned away from me, you cried
and I knew helplessness.

I wanted you to stop talking to yourself, so you could
come home. But you didn't. They sent you to the
Lakehead and your letters grew shorter and shorter. The
voices have never stopped. Even now when you visit I
hear them late at night. Just faint whispers trailing
off into sleep. And the rage grows on in me. Looking
out a window and remembering those days makes me
shudder and even the brightest day seems like a
darkness. Both of us have been battered along the way
not sure how two bodies start as one. Life is a
separation. Letters intensify it, put words to the
shadows that pass in front of us. Still we write
because that is how we can react safely and still cope
with the visits. Faces in photographs shrink.

LETTER IX

In the next room Breanne is drawing a picture of you.
She calls the guest room "Mama's" room. Sometimes she
likes to stand in the middle of it and imagine
you there behind her. She already knows the delicate
image of morning, and the distance families take on.
She wants to phone you, thinks that you are just down
the street visiting a friend. She can say Winnipeg, but
it's just another word that adults use to frame an
experience. Even 700 miles can fit into a head.

I still use your recipe for salmon loaf. Place its
molded form on the table and think of you near a mirror
your face quivering in the glass. Across the table, I
can see you sit nervously as though transported from
another planet. I am alone, the fork already rests on
my lip. Winter sky already dark.

This city is heavy today, a thin smoke floats above the
houses. In traffic I hear a song you sang to me as a
child, Hank Williams' voice turns suddenly into yours.
I smile at the driver in the car beside me as though he and I
were passengers in the miraculous. I want to get out
tell him my life story show him pictures I took of you
last summer and say that's her on the radio. But he
turns away embarrassed by the intimacy of my stare. I
turn the radio louder, move the car slowly through
traffic driving into the rest of my life with a smile
on my face. The whole city hears your song, hears it
for the first time as only you could sing it.

I can never say goodbye because that never is. In our photos we are either sitting or standing. The camera exaggerates the contours of our faces. Together we glow even in the small eye of the camera. Glow as only the living can. When the camera has closed itself for good, the glow remains, allowing us to turn away unafraid.

LETTER X

I remember one morning your wet face near my cheek as
you knelt to wake me. You then turned back to the wood
stove to put on the kettle and I heard this distant
future I now write from. I know that I am neither in
that bed nor here writing. You move in some unconnected
way, move through the house with no shadow. I imagine
that I am waking you, that my face is wet from an early
morning swim in the lake. Instead of bending over, I
shout your name, a name I can hardly pronounce, my mouth
full of water. I hear a bird plunge out of the sky.
When I move to the stove, the fire is dead, the stove
unused in 10 years, the metal slowly collapsing inward.

LETTER XI

When was it that we stopped writing? Why? Did the words
start to sound the same? Perhaps the words were playing
with us, changing their meanings in the mail so that
neither could trust what the other said. Tenderness can
not be discussed or claimed. The words owe us nothing
and everything, Mother. A place to begin, a place to
fall in love, a place to imagine your mother's face
when it is too late to call, a place where truth is
more than the echo of a sad song.

There were mornings I would spring out of bed and you
would be making me tomato soup for breakfast. And I
didn't see it then, didn't see how big a hole we had to
fill, didn't see how you had so little say over your
place in the world, didn't see how the madness grew
slowly one day after the other. At school, I could hear
you rocking in your arms at home wailing for hours
while the sunlight moved gently across your face. I
could feel your words enter my head and not leave.
Mornings were never the same: twisting themselves madly
into evening.

Saying goodbye on the front doorsteps, I don't go in
until your taxi is nearly across the city. Inside, you
still sit where I left you, and I cross over to you,
and both of us turn with mouths open to face the only
window in the room.

LETTER XII

You withdrew slowly, turning away with a smile as the
sun passed suddenly like a scream. I couldn't see you
breaking. Just one morning you were ironing and then
you collected your three children as though they had to
be shielded from what only you could see. On the
highway, you flagged down a blue car, and huddled near
the door cursing while the driver tried to make small
talk. I couldn't open my mouth, couldn't address his
attempts to be polite. My lips trembled and I turned
towards the passing landscape, usually familiar and
safe but now transformed into an anguished blur. It
wasn't you I turned to or my torn father standing at
the curb in shock, it was the sky with its grey face at
the car window. I tried to open the window but
couldn't. My brother and I did not speak, stared
straight ahead, tried to figure out if it was a
nightmare or not.

Dad followed us into town in his 51 Ford. Later at the
court house he and the doctor spoke in whispers. I felt
the world explode with their delicate murmurs. I wanted
them to tell me what to do, how to choose, as though my
whole life depended on what I did next. You spoke and I
tried to believe your words, see my father's face the
way you described it. However, all I could do was bend
with this new world, accept its twisted smile. That
morning I was born, oldest son trying to forge it all
back together. Going home in an April rain while my
mother wrestled with god in a jail cell. My father
unable to face himself in the mirror to shave. I
couldn't speak to him, hated the doctor's perfect calm

as he led us away from the court house. You standing
at the curb, hands cuffed not seeing me disappear from
your life as though I were never born. Sometimes later
you would deny that I was your son would lie softly and
claim that god was your husband, and you were here to
watch over us because our real mother had run away. And
I was scared that maybe it was true, that maybe I would
never be born, that I could never be anyone's son
again. Dad would not speak but faces the world since as
if it were trying to tear out his guts.

Down the street an elderly woman sells boxes of oranges
in January and I am tempted to buy one and peel each
orange to determine the degree of ripeness, to find the
seeds that will not go away, that surrounded by all
that flesh will still not flourish, but end as garbage.
All day I think of nothing but oranges, see them in the
windows, replacing the sun.

LETTER XIII

If after waking, we still do not wake, what then? You
stand, in a plain dress, near a window, waving. That is
how I awake some mornings and we are together, your
smile draws open the membranes of sleep. When I get out
of bed, you are gone. Nothing left but the faint
sparkle of your shadow on the wall. I look to see where
your hands are placed, run to a photograph to see your
face, study the size of your nose, the direction of
your eyes. Still I do not see, do not wake, roam around
in sleep like the last passenger on a midnight bus. At
the bedroom window, I can see the city stretch like a
fleeing army and still I do not wake, can't bring
myself to the surface, like a drowning man with one too
few breaths. What can I expect in waking, except that
the separation is forever, that I have never really
left the terror behind, that outside this sleep there
is nothing else?

LETTER XIV

In the slough's dark water, I learned to swim. You
would watch from the shore and later you would slide
gracefully into the water. You would show me how you
could float in that brown water without moving a limb.
However, when I tried it my feet sank slowly until they
touched the oozing mud bottom.

Sometimes mallards would circle the slough and land
around us, speaking to you as though they were used to
it. They would read your eyes and then suddenly take
flight again, moving as they usually did to another
slough or the lake across the highway. I would not have
been surprised then if you had lifted off too, followed
them as naturally as you rose from the water, new,
fresh, moving to the shore in slow calculated steps.
The towel wrapped around you made you look protected.

When we were swimming together, it was as though the
water were dreaming through us. Our minds slowed until
the water would not let us go. Hours later we would
emerge reborn. Our faces in the towels felt clean, the
air filled with the scent of jack pines. You would be
singing as you always were, looking towards the highway
not sure what any of it meant, not sure this was how
you wanted to begin again. I would follow to the
highway, swinging my towel toward the sky, feeling it dry
quickly in the summer heat.

At home, the bush stood at bay around the house. I
watched you making bread and wondered how we came, you
and I, to be so close to the edge of the earth.

LETTER XV

Some mornings you would see red serpents and I wondered
what that meant. Now I know it means that we never
completely see until we close our eyes and the world
shatters our sound-proof skulls.

We would sit on a dock on a hot summer's day and dangle
our feet in the warm lake water. And you would tell me
stories that began with "When I was young" "As a small
girl" and I would be mesmerized and frightened at the
same time. Afraid that under the lake, near our
dangling feet, large fish of various colours and forms
waited to pull us under. Nothing remains in my head now
except an image or two and those stories you told,
strange stories that never let go, that changed subtly
through time until they are true like everything else
that happened then.

Dad would take me fishing and you would wait at the
shore. Nothing but a small speck to us out in the
middle of the lake. I would wave to you, but you were
looking into the sun and singing to yourself.

The fish that we caught dad would clean while you and I
stood around the wood stove, trying not to hear the fish
scream.

The fish you invented so that your stories would belong
to me, would last past youth. Fish I can no longer eat
without feeling their songs in my throat, without
feeling my head beneath the surface of a lake.

LETTER XVI

I turn away as I take your picture, your face swollen
and frozen in the lens long after the shutter has
snapped you from this life. I put those pictures all
over the wall and look at them as I write this letter.
And it hurts the most to know that they will not last
are just patterns on paper, a lie I cannot face. The
sunlight always makes us adjust to it.

As a child, I sometimes would get caught in a snow
drift and I would cry for you to come out of the house
and rescue me. I knew then that sometime I would stand
at the mouth of your grave and would see only darkness
even on a cool fresh morning. You would come through
the knee-deep snow to lift me out. Your breath near my
face melted the ice on my eyebrows and I could see
again and feel the warmth that we formed. Our lives
stitched together despite the choices we could never
make but always made.

Slowly we become the letters we still write inside us.

SOMETIMES YOU WAKE AFRAID

SOMETIMES YOU WAKE AFRAID

Sometimes you wake at night afraid
and I hold you, trying to share
your fear but I am not there,
I am just heat on the other side of the bed.
Even when you call me I am not there,
my body confuses you, its weight everywhere.
I am a ghost, empty, burning undercover
like the shadows of past lovers.

When I awake afraid at night, hearing the wind rip
paths across the roof, I lie silent,
my body feeling cold as I grip
the side of the bed:
I turn to you and you are there warm and close
breath as sweet as the first flower I knew.

WHO IS THINKING THIS POEM?

It was a red carnation you first brought home.
In its small dream of water, its bloom
lasted for several weeks. Its red glow, alone,
was enough to light the entire room.
Which of us was first to wake
with its red pollen on our lips?
Which of us will be the one to take
it out to the garbage like the carcass

Of a bird we had for lunch? When it is gone
will you or I bring another, a hyacinth, perhaps,
or a rose, its petals falling one by one?
Neither of us able to watch its collapse.
Neither of us able to face the despair
when the flowers stop being there.

LANDING IN RAIN

All night a branch against the window kept you awake.
I heard you toss the covers on the floor.
The rain, nearly on your face, broke
on the skylight above us, splattered into vapours.
I fought sleep, pretended that morning is a sleeve
of a coat that I can't take off.
I knew the rain wouldn't stop until it was inside
or we left for work not looking ahead or behind.

When I see you at work, hair wet, eyes sore,
I know I should have held you last
night and put my mouth where the rain was,
and moved it slowly to the downpour's
pulse. Instead I slept without sleeping
the rain shaping my dreams all night.

ENGAGING MIGHT

God can play music but doesn't, turned amateur
as he has, music hastens the fire in his throat.
He is a costume we try on, not sure
how the sleeves should hang on the coat.
He doesn't pardon us or beg when we turn away
doesn't care if we are responsible or show up
when needed or if we move our erotic tongues as we pray,
or if we stand outside a church and let it blow up.

God ignores the heat, and is tone deaf
can't discern a note from a treble clef,
Holds his lips around a saxophone
no more tenderly than a dog renders a bone.
He stays in the band to hear groupies sigh
as they whet their tongues on his thigh.

SO DISTANT, SO NEAR

I hold you to protect you from harm
for a few minutes after the alarm.
Morning full of our bodies
the scent of last night's rain
passes quickly through the room.
I rise out of bed ready for work
uncertain of the ways I have hurt
you. Leave you still asleep,
covers at the foot of the bed in a heap.

In traffic, I forget the sink that won't drain,
the visitors that arrived last night.
The weather doesn't help with its endless rain.
During the night your moans gave me a fright.
Your tongue so smooth and sudden in my ear,
Morning so distant and so near.

TO YOU

When I am home alone, I feel I can talk to you.
Out shopping you don't care if I approve
don't care if I watch you or like the way you move.
You pose for a mirror thinking of me, too.
A small hat on your head, the sales clerk reminds
you of your mother. It is alone that I find

you. Your voice echoes pleasantly inside me
your hair with a touch of silver lies across my arm.
Your freckles fading the nearer you are and we
are different together, nothing left we can harm.
When I hear you at the door, I hide for a moment, afraid
that it is not you at the door, but someone I've made.

HEALING

There is a place our sighs never achieve
and you are in the middle of a large bed
your calm face makes me see and believe
that love is not what we hold in our head.
It moves us toward
something we don't really think about.
Our mouths fill with sentences
too hard to speak or shout.

Your feet softly circle in the air
as your eyes stay closed in their bunkers
the room so quiet we can't feel ourselves there.

Are there many other houses
like this where lovers feel
love wound and then heal?

ONE NIGHT IN SPRING

We sang songs until our throats grew raw
then undressing in the dark we folded our arms
around one another, our bodies sweating and small.
Your tongue was a window open on a hot night.
The moon was the face of a god staring
at us for hours trying to make enough light
to see our bodies as they took over our heads and
did not listen when we said stop. It felt
as though we were living our whole life in one night.

Sometimes your sighs would be above me others below
and your back arched like a tree on the windiest day.
Through the house there was a silent, slow
moan. Few things from that night lasted until
summer only the scar of the moon is on the bed still.

LISTENING AT DOORS

On a beach, the tide is full, and the wind
breaks the sea's music open so it falls forward
into our lap. Sea salt glistens on your thin
arm, and I think of the number three (its hard
backside pressed against the number that follows).
The sea doesn't know how we dream of it, smell
its delicate breath across our face, hear it bellow
its harsh melody. We are its rhythm, small

enough to be significant. Breanne plays on the beach
as though the apocalypse was a time of day that has
already passed. Her face turned to us is brave as
any I've seen. Young enough, she can still reach
for herself. We don't stop her but watch as parents will do
watch as the sea brings her back to us too.

A GUST INSIDE A GOD
- Rilke

Why do I think of god as a wind
at all since his green face is no different
from mine or yours. His arm not a limb
from a tree, his back not bent,

His fingers not severed by a lover's teeth.
God is not a man with better clothes or a woman
who knows that her hands are trembling beneath
a yellow coat. Yet I look for her omens

On every street, look for her eyes in a store window
listen for her breath at night near my ear.
I listen for a wind that builds all night to crescendo.
God knows what I anticipate, what I fear.
Without some calming finale perhaps I would no longer
believe in what she does to my sleep at night
or that each day begins with a fright,
god nothing but a sighing that gets stronger.

PERFECT ALTERATIONS

You are exquisite I think
and having thought that I know
that it is wrong that as I blink
you change near the window

thinking of a lover or friend
who is not so demanding or cruel
at times. Perfection ends
when we finally leave its school.

Your perfect smile contradicts me
and again I search for the impossible
hope that the ordinary is gone for good.

As lovers we have not understood
what we wanted, instead we are suggestible
at night growing old in front of a TV.

BREAKING AND ENTERING

Its so quiet that even the glass breaks
without a sound. Near the kitchen the cat
is devouring a helpless mouse. My hat
is tilted over my bald spot and shakes
as I try to find the cat's footprints
in the snow. Near the window something growls
and I can't imagine how death could
be so slow. Suddenly the cat howls

because I stepped on its toe
and I bring up in my hand the twisted
carcass of the mouse and toss it out
between the splinters of glass in the window.
We all feel warm even as we are dying. Our remains
cool slowly in a new morning's sudden burst of rain.

EXERCISES IN THINKING

A saxophone's notes are muffled in this room.
By noon the sunlight through the window can warm
your arm. Some mornings I chase the cat with a broom
but it is me I frighten more than her.
Hearts are the only thing we can hear beating.
Two of them synchronized all day long
At night, with the lights on
We feel like fish in an aquarium

Visible to everyone who passes by.
We can see some turn away from our
bludgeoned faces in the window.
We search through the kitchen for a power
switch or a device we could use to slow
the aging that fills us with weariness
and forms this open wound we try to dress.

PLAYING MUSIC

Do you feel the music slowly work its
way through your head until even your mouth
is swollen with it? It wakes you quick
from your dreams before completion. Without
music you never sleep for that long,
always dreading morning's slow explosion.
Some days you wake with a song
in your head you haven't heard before

Playing itself even still
deeper into your life. Notes spill
into your conversations. Followed by music
you can only listen and sway and feel sick.
With each note your life unravels and as you fear
is lost forever in someone else's ear.

AFTER SPRING

It is after spring that we awake
and are made, sweet bodies that break
open with sighs and breath
and know at birth about death.
Each morning we are the seasons
that we wake in or decease in.
I show you my tongue and then turn
away not sure what you will learn.
In spring we listen to the trees
in summer we sleep in the songs of bees.
In fall we hold our fingers in our
mouths. By winter we are flowers
without wings or mouths or windows.
By then our screams won't let us go.

The seasons repeat and so do we.
Coming to rest only long enough to be
disgusted by the way our bodies fail
until the seasons are merely a warm trail
we follow because without the changes
we would not know how a god arranges
our decline. Remember I love your neck the most
I hope someday we will be lovers even as ghosts.

A PRICE

There is a price we pay by listening
at night in the dark to sighs
we allow to linger in our swollen mouths.
We make poetry out of our thighs
our bodies not damaged by their work
or desire not changed too much
by our squeamish imagination. Others go berserk
but we do not, for we are still able to touch.

Embraced we lie perfectly still
while the night forms couplets around
us. Our small faces glow as our eyes fill
with the moon above. Every sound
we recognize but our own
as our singing escapes from this poem.

FINDING THE LIGHTS ON

THE PROBLEM OF SEEING
(After a day at the beach)

The problem of seeing is knowing
when to stop. What do you eliminate
because something reminds you of
the summer your father stripped bare
and dove off the dock into the lake
water settling above him forever
as he called from the shore behind you,
frightened of his new heights.

As you turned to him, life and death blurred
trees along the shore, were twisted from their roots
birds formed a black cloud above your head.
Your hands felt below the water for your body,
for a pocket of air to grasp.
Turning still, you fell into a dizzy dream.

Your father's hands reached beneath you
until there was air everywhere.
His mouth near yours as wet as eternity,
his lips a warm ring around you.
He dragged you towards the shore
calling to a distant figure there.
After lying in the sun for hours with
hands wrinkled from the water, you
watched your father back his old
ford slowly towards the water as though
preparing to tow the lake away.
Instead he folded it into the trunk, bucket by bucket.
Stopping to look past you towards your
mother waving on the beach
her feet pushed beneath sand.

When your father finally drove away
his car changed shape and colour every few feet.
Cigarette after cigarette butted into his ashtray.
He left you on the beach with your mother
watching the dust settle on the road.
Your mother and father are figures too near the water.

After a day at the beach, there is only destruction.
Buildings torn from your life as though
struck by a tornado. Cars decay in minutes
clothes burn in closets. After a day at the beach,
you are no longer young: your parents move out,
taking their furniture, clothing.
Your feet stay wet all night no matter
how many times you dry them.
You leave the window open
with hopes of hearing their return
your father's car grinding across the gravel.
The all-night disk jockey plays songs
your parents used to sing.

(The next day at the beach, your father is still
swimming; his breath forming small waves on the water.
Your mother is searching for shells
to put on the dresser.
You are a teenager hiding in the water
waiting for your friends with new cars,
waiting for your body to turn beautiful.

Out over your head,
you try to find the shore again with your feet.
Discovering who you are one cell at a time.
No one comes to rescue you.
Boats pass too far away to hear you, to see your
father swimming in a circle around this spot).

A SHAMAN SINGS OPERA TO HIS BRIDE

As though a song was what love came wrapped in
a marvel that made women love men because
men were so much better at tasting the world.
Libretto or some other words coming from behind tight lips.

It might be in Niagara Falls or in Victoria
from the hotel window where the bride can see
water, in every direction water
she hesitates there as though selecting
the right place to drown.

The shaman takes something made out of rubber
from his pocket and plays it like a mouth organ.
The bride sits on the bed as though she were seasick
The shaman falls out a window and flies over the water
like a giant dove, his arms pushing the sky beneath him.

The bride waves from the window not knowing whether
to laugh or cry. She is not yet comfortable with
magic. When the shaman returns she is reading a book
her fingernails biting into the pages.
She doesn't love the shaman or really care if he has returned.
She loves stories and wants to write them.

Music is what the shaman used to persuade her
to marry him and now she distrusts anything
that has rhythm. Later she will learn to love
without her body, learn how to touch another
beneath skin and bones.

Tonight she will not sleep with the shaman but
will wait in the dark for the world to stop singing.
When the shaman rises she will be gone, have caught a bus
to Toronto or Vancouver, some place where the shaman cannot
find her. On the streets she will learn what power is. She will
stop listening for a man to undress himself into her life.
Becoming a bride has freed her from doing that again.
In the days ahead, she will discard certain words,
invent others to fill the gaps and if years later
she runs into the shaman by chance or on purpose
she will sing opera into his narrow ear,
his voice no longer capable of such beautiful sounds.
That is what marriage means, music the first
power that we recognize. Sleeping with someone to
open our bodies permanently.

WAIST DEEP

They are baptized in a lake in mid-summer
because it is easier than getting married.
He holds her like a man confused by his body.
She gets into the car opens a window and spits
out her gum. The back seat of the car is littered
with candy wrappers. She fidgets with the radio
hopping about as he drives. With her head out the window
she catches her future in the face, turns to
the boy at the wheel and wonders how his body
can be so still. He doesn't see her lower her head
in tears. All he wonders is how to keep his
hands from trembling on the steering wheel
how to stop from turning to her while he drives.
Their lives like the radio antennae extend
into future picking up random signals.

She was my mother afraid of the water, afraid
my father might not understand her ways.
He understands metal better than flesh, is more
comfortable with a carburetor than a breast.
When he drinks, he becomes wicked and that shocks her.
Some mornings, he lies crumpled in a ball
in bed, unable to face her body, unable to
break through her strangeness.
All day she sits near a window, while she
carries me inside, sits and wonders
how her body could betray her like this.
Like her mother, she spends hours at the piano
her fingers following the notes in her head.

He is tentative, uncertain how to express himself.
His thick glasses grow thicker each year
and building her a house seems to do no good.
Their children hold them hostage with their vulnerability.

In the morning, she listens to the radio
and feeds me pablum while my father cuts
trees all day, moving the axe with confidence.
At night he can hardly speak has lost his words
during the day, looks at his coffee, as though
it represented the rest of his life.
She can hear him drink, feel his lips nestle
near the rim of the cup, and she is more alone
then, wanting to stand up and walk away, turn
down the street and vanish. Instead she puts
the dishes away and turns out the lights.
Listens to his breathing near the wall.
Long slow breaths that sound like a clock
chopping up her life. Her hands along
her body warmly part her legs and reach inside.
Her hazel eyes glowing lightly in the dark.
In the morning, they wake separate; my mother
rising early to feed me, her teeth
yellow in the mirror next to her red lips.
My father stays alone in bed until the sun
reaches his cheek through the window.
That is the way they both started to go crazy
unable to control the twitches of their bodies,
unable to kiss the other's trembling fist.

My mother started to talk to herself
while she played the piano, started
to go crazy in the shacks my father built her.
Lonely in the middle of the day she would
cry and hide in music. They moved farther from town,
as if pursued by changes they could not understand.
They stopped making love, stopped having children.
Learned to dream for us instead, tell us
the stories they couldn't share with anyone
else even each other. My father drank,
swore and buried his pride near
my mother's pillow. He lifted his eyes to heaven:
the last place he dared to look.
She taught me to write songs, to hear the music
even in a burning house, to hear as father
slipped in late at night stumbling through the house,
waking everyone with his drunkenness.
Now I dream with them, help them get off
a train, help them move the few small boxes
they have left. In the end they gave everything
else away. They are together still leaning against
each other for support, barely making it through
each day. Baptizing all those years ago didn't help.

VOICES CARRY

When I was young voices would carry
for hours across the small lake
near my house. Many long summer nights
I would spend covered in sweat, while
down the lake tourists married themselves
to the wilderness, and crossed the lake
in large boats, swam naked. Their voices
carried across the lake like the slow notes
from a church choir. I was drawn to those voices
and would swim across the bay to get closer
to them. I listened carefully to their slang,
the long sound of their vowels. They laughed as though
paradise could be this simple. After dark
they dressed in the trees and drove away, slowly,
as though they were leaving their life behind.
As I watched from the middle of the bay, I could see
their tail lights glow briefly and then vanish.
Below the surface of the water, my body trembled.
I swam to the wrong shore, right into their heads.

I was as much a tourist as they were. The only
difference was I had no place to return to
after the thrill of summer had passed.
This bush didn't belong to me or anyone.
Sometimes I even felt my body was a violation
as it glided through the water. Yet I was
too old to swim away, too young to stay.
On each of those nights left alone in the water,
without expecting to ever reach a shore
I continued to swim and as I swam
I became older, my body beginning to
leave me as I approached the shore. Panting on the

sandy beach, I could hear new voices not coming
from across the water but from within, voices
that cursed the sound the water made on the sand,
that cursed the horse flies that droned around me.
The trees bent in a soft wind, turned
away from the lake as though about to chase after
the last few rays of daylight. In this older body,
I could nearly stop breathing my lungs so full
of air. The tourist now long gone, in hotels or
cabins on other lakes, their voices falling
against plaster or wood walls, echoless.

In the available light, I would return to the lake
move my hands through the water as though
searching for the residue that time may have left.
The tepid water felt comfortable and eerie.
In the sand my feet sank, as though seeking a resting
place. The last tourist on the beach, I would wave
to myself still out in the water listening,
trying to find his own voice, trying to discover
the right moment to begin screaming.

Today, neither young nor old, I am the one in the car
who doesn't look back but drives following
the timid aim of the headlights. In my windshield,
I see nothing but the remains of bugs and
a reflection of the lake far behind me now.
There is no one listening, no one waving
from the water, presumably drowning.

The inside of the car is warm, pleasantly scented,
like a hearse. North of here the northern lights already
fill the sky. The headlights wildly jump up and down
as I try to follow the winding road.
Suddenly above the radio and the dull moans
of the car engine I can hear a scream. I don't
need to look back, I know what is taking place.

WHAT YEAR WAS THAT?

You can hear your mother cry again
hear the night hiss as it passes,
hear your father cough, bending a leg
in his sleep as you listen near his window.
He dreams your hand upon the bed
dreams your mouth above him like a small moon,
dreams your mother awake in her room, windows
breathing, her mother next to her on the piano
her hair grey with threads of moonlight, she
tries Beethoven, Bach, but nothing happens
the keys are frozen. Your mother screams out the window
at a car that passes too close, and her
wrinkled face is caught in the glass
a distorted expression staring back into the room.

Your father dreams your shoe is lost on the stair
while you move past his room, he calls out
names you've never heard, as you try
to open every window in the house.
In the kitchen, you drink a glass of milk
while it snows outside, and you can't hide
from the radio, as it plays some slow jazz.
The world changes a cell at a time,
through an open window you blow a kiss.
Each of us saves such a moment inside us forever.

SEEING THROUGH THE DISGUISE

i

Some mornings I forget the prairie's sadness. I look
across the city and see only mountains. The book in
front of me calls me back, calls me to face the tangle
of words, calls me to the edge of your bed. Your face
caught in the sunlight.

ii

Breanne is sick in the next room, and I smell the fruit
in the fridge rotting. The rain outside is calico: your
hand on the table. The poplars in the yard need
pruning. This is our first attempt at being in love.

iii

A boy passes selling chocolate or dirty magazines. His
father was a farmer or welder or mechanic in his other
life although he doesn't remember it now or his
homeland. Like my father, he poses as though he was
about to be sentenced. The boy passes our house and I
watch him. I listen for a faint explosion at the end of
the street.

iv

As I drive back from Banff, my headlights search for the
future. Between us the light passes like a sliver of
salvation. I could hear you cry all night. Could feel
your tongue break through the glass of your dream. The
car parked two blocks away.

v

I rented the suite in the basement to my father's ghost.
We get along fine, careful not to speak to one another.
You approve of his quiet ways. During the day, he
sleeps, waits for twilight before turning on the TV.
Across the street, a girl watches me from her window.
Loneliness is the last word of every sentence.

vi

It's been snowing for a week but take no notice. If this
letter reaches you before I phone, I will call when it
doesn't arrive. Call mother for me and ask her why she
doesn't have my address. Put your head to her chest and
see if you can hear what I took with me when I left.
Show her my photographs. Tell me if she can see through
my disguise.

THE LONG WAY HOME

You take the long way home
because that means you arrive late
and will not have to be alone. Looking in a window,
you see your father motionless staring at
the place he last saw your mother.
You wait for the right moment to walk in.
The sun across your back, your hands move through
the air like an axe, your father
stands up suddenly and holds you.
Every other room in the house is
empty and you are frightened.
Your mother is in a vase on the mantlepiece.
Sometimes her face appears in the window
calling you as though heaven was only
a few streets away. Your father
sings a song while you lie on the floor.
His back to you like a magician.
Sometimes his face shrivels in the sunlight
and you turn away and call your mother's
sweetness from a dream, place her pale face
in front of you while she walks around
you as though you were a statue
she was trying to finish. You know that life
is a sickness that turns us inside out,
that makes fathers become lonely
their hands pushed inside them,
their faces etched out of flesh
as though dipped in acid. Mothers are
transformed into dust and wake you in
the morning with their loneliness.
Small boys taste death first
cover their bodies with lime and listen

as their skin hisses in the wind.
They are alone, unable to open their hands
always taking the long way home
unable to arrive first, unable to
sit in an empty house, their mothers
dead, sick, or away. Their own rooms
decorated as though they were constantly
in a state of grief or were afraid
to let their imagination out.
Inside, their organs are rotting away,
shrinking from their own amino acids.

.

CROSSING A SMALL BRIDGE (IN WINTER)

Once horses commanded this bridge
with dignity, moving aside pedestrians.
Those walking would have smelled
the horses passing and remembered
the warmth of that moment for a long time.
The bridge makes you stand back
think of a lover's form near you
calling from across the narrow water,
below. Water that is nearly all ice
but is always water, not changed
by the different things you call it.
Once on the bridge you are
an invisible shape in the web
of it. You are no longer able to turn
and run, or walk away, suspended
forever as though you were the bridge
the wood and metal invisible to everyone
else. Just you there above the water
reaching out like an angel or saint.
Bridges are not for crossing but for
looking out from for seeing where
your place in the world begins.

PLAY OF THE EYES
    - Elias Cannetti

He waited in his cocoon of rage.
He waited for those who would come early
and those who would come late. He waited
with blood drying on his hands. He waited
the quiet serene executioner. His hands were
the same as my father's hands, dirty
fingernails, knuckles swollen, fingertips
blunted by work. In the mirror he was
uglier than the death he would bring.

I can hear him still, every sunday
driving up and down the back alleys
searching for places to discard the dead.
Bodies dumped into the garbage as though
they were nothing but cigarette butts.
Could he hold his breath long enough
to avoid the stench, could he walk past
strangled children and not weep, could he
keep the rifle away from his mouth?
I can hear him climb the stairs
pause in the hall to finish a glass of water.
I can hear him take the rope from his pocket
as though it were a wedding tie.
Did he suppress a cough before he entered their room,
check himself to avoid discovery? Grandfather
executioner in his green shirt come for
the young first. Did he watch the play of their eyes

as each died with not enough air left inside to form
a single scream, each unsure of how to wake
from this kind of nightmare? When he left their
room, did he look back uncertain of what he'd
done, uncertain of what was next, or of how
to stop it, knowing he was now alone forever?

I hear his dreams, the siren that
never comes. All night, he sat in front of the TV,
the dead around him no longer resisting.
Did the dead continue to breathe
unprepared for death, did he fear
that one of the children might sneak out
a window and call the police, did he creep back
upstairs for another look, eyes screaming
at him? The dark penetrating every inch of the house.

Later he surrendered, his image flashing
on the TV in the living room of the undiscovered dead.
He looks away from the camera as though he knows
that they are watching. Hating him even in death
waiting for the final revenge.
I hear the words the cameras do not record,
I hear him exhaust his fear without being freed.
He knows that there will be no moral,
that justice will never be served,
he is alive and they are not. Each victim must
have twitched violently while he watched.
For some their hatred kept them alive longer
refusing his final command as long as possible.

He has no one to command now, no one to
march to death. Even if he doesn't know it
yet he is dying, nothing can stop that.
Any sentence handed out will be incomplete.
I will never hear him weep or see him
surrender, it's taken him this long to realize the terror
nothing will free him except the eyes he can no
longer look into, except the words he has no idea
how to say.

NO ONE CAN HEAR THE GRASS BURN

The young think that music does the trick.
Listening with ears blocked by an invisible will.
The agony between the chords
is numbed by the quiet of space.
We stand on the bones of others
as though they were bleachers.
Raised above everything the air is no clearer
the smells no better. Too many learn
too late by dying. Taking the truth
with them like an extra bag.
We stand at their graves and call out
but there is no answer
nothing but the sound of the
gravekeeper's lawn mower
a faint and humble dirge.

We wait for the wars to end sweetly
for lovers to again unite
their bodies warm and tender.
We wait for dreams that make sense
that we can wake from and finally
praise a god.

Don't you hear the future
unfasten itself from us?
Turn suddenly like a crazy wind
winding us further and further inside.
We pretend that there is some
faraway country where someone is working it out
where sensible people can hear the grass burn
feel their lives fill with smoke.

Where the jungle is deepest others hide
colouring their faces with the pigments of nature.
Hold in their teeth some western instrument of power
smiling like the maddest person on earth
they will linger in the dream of death forever
watch themselves turn black in the small sun
listen to a strange music shape their movements
and for all of that we are certain
happy that somewhere a small spark survives
after us as though that is enough
to start a whole new world.

HELL AND SOME NOTES ON A PIANO

Thinking about hell, I sit down to play some song on the piano. The notes remind me of my death, the way the earth smelled fresh as rain. Music is the ultimate confusion, echoing through an empty house like the bruised light of a cloudy day. Even after I stop playing, the music continues, returning home, the notes reversed, a reflection in sound's mirror. Nothing could be worse than to hear the notes become the fuel of my anger. Fingers controlling the tone and texture. Music, the discard of gods, cruel and tender at the same time. The ebony keys lift out of their sockets and turn inside a skin of light. Only a scattering of notes is left, sounding discordant across a fading memory. Such was hell when I was young and still knew the piano.

BOY IN A CHOIR

It's not murder that brings him to this church. He wants to feel god's affection while standing on a wooden bench. Sometimes god is late too not arriving until the choir is nearly finished practising for the day. Late or not god is welcomed. The boy can see that god has stopped being holy years ago, that he listens to the conversations of sinners because he is more interested in the gossip than in salvation. Still he remains loyal to those he has abandoned. Even his clothes reflect neglect: his shoes worn through. The boy has heard lovers tiptoe from his mother's room at night and each of them walks like god, the slow and natural walk of a man satisfied in love. Leaving the choir practice each Sunday, the boy pauses near the grave of his father. He listens for a sound, any sound, but all he ever hears is the music of the children in the nearby playground. Still their music is so beautiful he wants to dance in someone's arms. The boy is not disappointed that god can bring little more than sleep to our lives. But when the boy sings in the church beside other boys and girls, he can feel his mother's arms around her lover slowly slacken, can see her turn to look out a window at the Sunday traffic. Nearly on tiptoes the boy reaches for the highest note in a hymn and as he does god slips out the side entrance and heads for the boy's house.

PROGRESS

Above Canmore, near the Spray Lakes, I sense
that we have climbed too far, and when we
reach our car below it will be someone
else's life I will be stealing. My father
points at a peak we are both too old to
reach. I forget that bodies weigh
more than the light. On the other
side of the peak, power lines hum.
The town site below us is the world
as we left it. Nestled between mountain ranges
waiting for the mountains to crumble.
This is the one moment in our two lives when
we are comfortable together. Neither of us can hear
how the other's head rings with a fear that
mountains make stronger.

This morning while leaving the city
we passed a field of crows. Their cries could not
penetrate the car's closed windows.
My father told me his life story, year by year
up to the day I was born. I could
sense, then, that we had both covered too
much ground. My foot on the accelerator was
heavy as though its placement determined
the rest of our lives. Now above the
highway, nearly above the trees, I know it's
impossible to find the right distance
between us. Each year we move back towards
our beginnings, when Father and son first
discovered each other. It could rain now
and I wouldn't notice, content to find my

place in this landscape, content to know
dreams are not this strange or complete. My
father wants to find wild animals here, a
squirrel, marmot, coyote: it doesn't
matter. He wants to make it to the top of
the trees before dark, and see the clouds
below him for the first time. I suspect
that he knows his limitations too well. I
blame the wild for keeping us apart, he
too comfortable there, I uncertain and
uneasy about my lack of control of it. I
suspect too that inside, both of us stopped
looking for our story. It is here above the
highway, animals out of view, the city
forgotten like a dream upon waking.

FORGETTING THE SMELLS

I am already forgetting the smells of June now
that August is ending. Down the street pumpkins
are lining the driveways. Once this was a city
where the sky listened to your thoughts and
angels could be seen at night with their
children. Now its simply full of suburbs where
cowards take off their clothes in dark rooms.
This was what heaven once was to us when we were
younger and didn't understand such things
clearly enough. Every house down this street
leans with some gentle imperfection and we do
not see it, see only the robust skyline around
us daylight full of darkness. Out of some houses
strangers are taken in handcuffs while in others
stereos or TVs sing to one another through thin
walls. Some mornings it feels as though we were
the transients in all this, that everything
continues to run whether we are here or not. In
back yards some people look at the blue sky on a
Saturday morning as though it contained some
scar they could not look away from. While they
sit, laundry tumbles through various cycles.
Nothing is original or real, merely the sad
predicaments of mysterious characters. Down the
street our children play with neighbours'
children and it seems that all along everything
was out of our control, the names supplied even
before we were born, our own children sitting
across from us at dinner know with a certain
cruelty that we can not answer their questions.

At the funeral of a friend's wife we feel the
emptiness we use to call god. A small microphone
sucks the voice of her daughter as she reads
some favourite poem. To us misery sounds long
and detailed. At the front of the room the
minister is tentative, not looking at anyone but
down the centre aisle where no one is sitting.
Our new cars or relatively new cars are parked
at the curb like hearses. In the morning in the
mirror we see nothing, our eyes torn out from
lack of sleep. Teeth rot gently beneath the
gums. In our cars we feel like targets, imagine
somewhere a mad man with a gun takes aim, but it
never happens. Each morning alive confirms what
we already know: that the breath is taken slowly
out of our lives. Off in the distance school
children wait as though our language were not
enough. Soon they will be at our throats like
wolves charging from the hills, not waiting to
see what love is in our eyes, merely tearing at
the flesh, tearing and wailing their madness
driven to a frenzy by the grunts of gods.
Dead. Dead.

ENDINGS

And my daughter, at breakfast, asks for more bacon,
    but leaves the table without eating it.
    Turning to her toys, she sings me a song.
    I hear your words in it.
And my father writes today for the first time
    asks me to send his income tax back,
    he wasn't sure how to sign his name.
And last night I forgot to listen for your breath,
    I fell asleep uncertain of the hour
    uncertain of the day.
And the winter here will not hide us. My daughter
    peeks through the door asking "what does
    winter do when it's tired?" I can't remember
    the answer, can't face her eyes through the door.
And the warnings never cease on labels, on the tv and radio,
    on airplanes, life savers. The warnings never cease
    but we stop reading them, stop listening, stop pretending
    that they can help.
And all last week I wanted to call you but didn't. Instead
    I read a few poems, thought about the last words you said,
    thought about throwing the dictionary out, thought about
    your laughter in the kitchen, thought about the starfish
    on your desk.
And my mother has stopped singing, her throat treated
    by a young doctor. All smiles, he persuades her to
    do breathing exercises. My mother has thrown out her
    stereo, fixes me breakfast as though there wasn't a train
    waiting for me, as though she could still taste the bacon.
And my parents live together inside me, talking all night
    while I listen. Nothing they say surprises me. That is how
    certain I am that none of this has happened.

And this is a warning how not to listen, how to believe
    I still love you can't think that, can't explain
    how your smile glows, how last night I fell asleep
    in the middle of my life and didn't listen.
And I have seen the dust, found out what life is from
    my daughter. Can you hear her now? She is searching for
    her mother; she shows me her fingers, sadness on her face.
    I can't begin to write her life, my ruin, she knows
    a sentence is all we dare construct together.

And I think about my grandparents' graves in Dryden
    I haven't been there since 1961 when my mother took
    me there just before she had to be sent away again.
    I want to go back to see if the names have withstood
    the years. Want to remember their faces, hear my mother
    call them, hear her sing their final hymn.
And some nights I can contain it no longer, dare not break out
    of this life, dare not scream from the balcony of our
    bedroom, dare not say the word "truth" without meaning it,
    dare not pronounce "reality" without leaving it,
    dare not look into your eyes without bringing love.
And in the morning after a rain, the roads are
    covered with frogs, their voices together louder than the end
    of the world. Logic is a small part of my life, it forces me to
    wait for you to wake, to stand at the top of the stairs and
    not jump.
And I write one last letter to my mother. In it I list my life
    in the margin I scribble dates and times. She writes back
    sending a new song she has written. She has a phone now
    and I call instead, never hearing her newest song,
    never correcting her spelling in my head.

And I blame myself because it is too quiet at night, because
   my daughter wakes with a cold, because I can't reach
   the end without looking back, without seeing the darkness
   in both directions, no one to stand with, no one to begin
   the dance.
And this is what a name sounds like, this poem
   is a loudspeaker, words ripple and avoid being words,
   nothing ends like language, nothing is so easy to play with
   to pretend it means just what we say.

GOD'S MOUSTACHE

God is the last voice we hear at night as he
practices his lines. When we finally see him it will
not be his moustache that bothers us but his bent
over posture as he walks. Light a cigarette I say and
lean against your reflection in the mirror. God has
no time to make order out of our chaos. He has no
time to listen while we lie to one another about
love. He is careful to ignore our mistakes to laugh
when we call him divine. He is sympathetic but
strong. When he is certain he will summon the wind
and carefully he will form our words with it. Seeing
us run he will know that infinity is lonelier than he
thought. When the wind finally lifts him above our
trembling voices he will number the universe for us
tossing bones at us to indicate the beauty he sees in
us. There is no name he will take or certain path he
will follow, his time amongst us exhausted before we
understand that power begins with forgetting.

DARK SNOW

Our daughter wants us to insert the wrong words into
her stories and she laughs when you read "The night
before Easter". Morning descends across our faces
slowly and our teeth find new flesh to bite. We all
want to hear new stories, to say "Fuck it" one night
when the sirens sound so close we run to the window. An
old girlfriend dies in a car accident and standing by
a mirror the light is broken by the glass. We tell
Breanne stories first not naming the figures who lurk
behind the characters who move their hands in the air
as though drowning. The stories are narrated by someone
who is not in them. We forget that there is blood spilled
in the stories and that some of the characters have
found the calm in their lives too late. Sometimes
Breanne doesn't listen; her memory turned off; I catch
her staring ahead and I know she has found the darkness
in the stories. Some nights we can't relax, restless as
though our bodies were off living in one of those
stories we are always reading. Sitting in opposite
chairs, one of us occasionally looks up but doesn't
speak and I feel as though it was our breathing alone
that kept the Earth spinning. I think of you naked
beside me my tongue twisting your hair and I feel the
music of your pulse on my neck. I realize how long it
has taken for us to recognize ourselves and each other.
Our story no one sings in lullabies or whispers to a
child. We move through the pages, the words nothing but
artifacts we discard along the way. We are protected by
the warmth and by the tension beneath our skins.
Everything in its place; everything broken and in
disarray. Some evenings you ask: "Are we falling?" and
I see two figures dancing as they fall. On each face
there is a smile.

Their bodies are calm and relaxed. I am small, I think,
turned around at every corner, imagining that the wind
speaks to me at night, its breath nearly breaking the
window. When Breanne falls downstairs I scream and
catch a horrified glimpse of my swollen face in the
mirror. Some day the sun will stop shining, soon the
moon may abandon its lovers, but we know that coming
home at night, a head full of stories, one of us will
stop for milk, the other will wait in the kitchen
thinking of a certain night we were alone. That is how
we speak through walls, across rooms, you upstairs, me
down. The first night we spent together nearly
forgotten but still there beneath the surface
noticeable in the way we do things together smiling
across the room waving as the other departs identifying
the other in our thoughts, nothing broken, nothing joined
we are made by mistakes, by breathing into small rooms
teeth against tongue, elbows bent like a disarmed
weapon. Nothing forgotten, not the heat, not the cold
nothing except everything, the way you sing, the way you
lift Breanne from the car. It is all there not traceable
to any other particular moment in our lives. The danger
of the dark snow goes unnoticed, moving from car to
building and back, we live this way, telling our daughter
stories, changing the ending each time and not sure why.
She listens and pretends not to notice smiles when we
leave the room and gently close her door. We supply the
details because we are supposed to or because we like
to but it doesn't matter to her, she only wants
the stories to last longer so she can finally find out what
it is she has missed.

NECESSARY FICTIONS

The sunlight falls across your face and bleeds
its way through the doorway and onto the bed
in the next room. Without looking, I know
where your socks are, where the bed sits
sagging nearly to the floor. As the
sunlight continues through a hundred different
houses we talk slowly, our mouths only opening wide
enough to suck more air. Few of us want
to think of death on a Saturday when the shopping
is almost done. At the meat counter, I see a
package of chicken livers and I think of your
old house and the last night we both spent there.

Who will watch as I pass my hand across your
shoulder, smell the smoke from your last cigarette?
When I was younger, I wanted to know what stories you
carried with you, but you never said. You just listened
instead, absorbing everything your son uttered, giving nothing
back, not speaking for whole days or weeks. I wrote
everything down, then thought that my life was
the summation of all words it used. I would
watch you eat eggs in the morning, the sun not up
yet. From my small bedroom, I listened as you hummed
something under your breath. I could never make it
out and after a while I was convinced that I was
never meant to, as if to know that would be to know
too much. Even now I can't say I really understand,
or know the difference. Sometimes in the morning
we behave like moths in front of an expensive light.
Still we can't say the words that will stop a family
from coming apart. Your bruised face stares
across at me during breakfast and I have lost

the necessary fictions, the ones that
keep us from coming apart in each other's arms.
We behave as many fathers and sons do.
Something makes us linger here, something drives us
into these oddly shaped rooms together.

Here is a father disinclined to speech,
here is a son not yet able to listen with his mouth.
When we see each other we see who we are
or who we will be when we are able to break across
the barriers and become joined as dust
in the mouth of a shovel. The sunlight will
not extinguish itself, we must do it, must close our
eyes and look away, look down a dark hall towards
where someone is sleeping.

QUIET RAGE

There is a fire across the street. Fire trucks arrive in
succession. You feel the pulse of the window against
your forehead as you watch the flames move into the sky
as though they were following your thoughts. The light on
your face flickers and standing alone in this small
room you understand the care a god has made in placing
you here. No one: not your daughter sleeping
downstairs: not your wife alone in the bed upstairs:
not the bystanders across the street can hear your
heart slow down and speed up at this moment or see your
hands move over your face, shaping and reshaping its
features. You are a figure alone in a room, historical,
and fantastic, existing and not existing as the night
proceeds regardless. You are afraid that the living and
dead are not that different in their predicaments. The
fire next door leaves you cold and for a moment you
want to stay awake forever, don't want to leave this
moment when you understand the extent of your
breathing.

You move to the stereo. Soon your head fills with
guitars and organs and for a moment you hum along as
you return to the window to check on the fire. There is
only a faint glow now as four or five firemen move
through the debris on the lawn. Near the corner of the
house you see someone standing and for a moment it
looks like you or your father, someone so familiar you
can't recognize him. Rubbing your face against the
window you feel the cold of the glass penetrate. The
singer on the stereo is whistling now and the figure

across the street turns shyly away and stares at the
shell of the house and you can feel the tears run down
his cheek, know that he can't turn around without
being emptied.

Plain and noble words we choose to begin our life
stories. The rage has dissipated and it is late enough
now that you dare go back to bed. You turn nothing off,
not the lights or stereo, but move slowly away from the
window, not looking back once, knowing that in the
morning your daughter will ask about the fire and you
will be helpless then, searching through the paper for
details as though you had slept through it all too.

The light in the kitchen will brightly bounce off the
chrome fridge. You will not lie to her but will tell
her the fire was not something you dreamed last night.
No, it was something you had to watch because in it you
saw the endless flicker of your anguish, saw the
sadness on the firemen's faces as they worked, it was
something you had to get up to watch so that you could
learn how to grow old. Learn how to love and how to
save the beautiful for the morning.